DATE DUE

NO. 59

UNIVERSITY OF MINNESOTA PAMPHLETS
ON AMERICAN WRITERS   65 CENTS

Caroline Gordon

BY FREDERICK P. W. McDOWELL

PAMPHLETS ON AMERICAN WRITERS • NUMBER 59

UNIVERSITY OF MINNESOTA

Caroline Gordon

BY FREDERICK P. W. McDOWELL

UNIVERSITY OF MINNESOTA PRESS • MINNEAPOLIS

Printed in the United States of America at the
Jones Press, Minneapolis

Library of Congress Catalog Card Number: 66-64592

PUBLISHED IN GREAT BRITAIN, INDIA, AND PAKISTAN BY THE OXFORD
UNIVERSITY PRESS, LONDON, BOMBAY, AND KARACHI, AND IN CANADA
BY THE COPP CLARK PUBLISHING CO. LIMITED, TORONTO

CAROLINE GORDON

FREDERICK P. W. McDOWELL, a professor of English at the University of Iowa, is the author of the books *Ellen Glasgow and the Ironic Art of Fiction* and *Elizabeth Madox Roberts,* as well as many articles on British and American literary subjects.

Caroline Gordon

CAROLINE GORDON's work is more impressive in its totality than each book seemed to be on publication. The result has been that only recently have critics felt the full impact of her work and been able to see its unity. No full-length study has yet appeared despite the subtlety and strength of her talent. Her fiction is now securing some of the respect due it, however, with the popularity in university circles of her critical books, *The House of Fiction* and *How to Read a Novel*.

Caroline Gordon was born October 6, 1895, at Merry Mont farm near Trenton in Todd County, Kentucky, close to the Tennessee border. Here "Black Patch" tobacco is the main crop, so called because it needs to be fired to darkness in curing. This region forms the setting for many of Miss Gordon's short stories and all her novels except *Green Centuries* and *The Malefactors*. *The Garden of Adonis* and "Her Quaint Honour," for example, contain many details of tobacco growing, and references to local agriculture abound in her work. Her early writing reflects many of the same beliefs held by the group of writers known as the "Agrarians," who declared their principles in *I'll Take My Stand* (1931). She felt, as they did, that the hierarchical society of the early South was preferable to the social disintegration she saw in North and South alike. Modern chaos, the Agrarians contended, resulted from the prevalence of a scientific cast of mind and a mechanized culture, from the decay of a feudal relationship between landowners and workers on the soil, and from the loss of spiritual certitude. In tendency Miss Gordon was Agrarian as she began her career, and she tried through her fiction to offset the empiricism, skepticism, and impersonal aspects of an industrial society.

Directly or by implication she has always celebrated the stability to be found in the southern past and the dynamic quality of personal relationships at their best. Her earlier novels, which stressed the need for both social hierarchy and individual responsibility, are Christian "in hope," in the same sense that she once used this term to describe the fiction of the unorthodox Henry James. More recently, she has turned to Christianity as a redemptive force in a fissured age. In her two latest novels, however, she continued to value an ordered social existence and a sympathetic understanding between human beings even while she became increasingly Christian in emphasis.

Her own heritage encouraged respect for the southern tradition. Her mother's ancestors, the Meriwethers, came to Kentucky from Virginia in the eighteenth century; the early phase of this migration forms the subject of *Green Centuries*. Her father, James Morris Gordon, arrived in the 1880's as a tutor for the Meriwethers. From his love of the classics and his passion for sport, Miss Gordon was to derive her complete knowledge of these two facets of southern culture. Recollections of her father form the animating source of *Aleck Maury Sportsman*. Like Aleck Maury, James Gordon conducted a boys' school — in Clarksville, Tennessee — which emphasized the classics, history, and mathematics; and for some years Miss Gordon attended this school. Only later, in her teens, did she regularly attend public schools. In 1916 she graduated from Bethany College, which thirty years later awarded her an honorary degree.

After she completed college, Miss Gordon taught for three years in high school and then turned to journalism. As a reporter for the *Chattanooga News* from 1920 to 1924, she reviewed the Fugitive poets and got to know many of the Agrarians. She became the wife of one of them, Allen Tate, in November 1924. The marriage was a happy and understanding relationship, although it ended in divorce in 1959. Association with Tate enabled Miss Gordon to define her theory of fiction and the kind of novel she wanted to write. This relationship resulted in the joint editorship of *The House of Fiction* with its incisive discussions of literary theory and, more important, she was encouraged to devote herself, without dissipation of her energies, to the artist's career.

The Tates went to live in Paris in 1928 when he was awarded a Guggenheim Fellowship, and they stayed abroad until 1930. In Paris Miss Gordon wrote and gave final form to *Penhally*. In 1932 she herself received a Guggenheim award and was enabled to compose *Aleck Maury Sportsman* and the short stories which have Maury as their protagonist. After 1930 the Tates settled for some years at Benfolly farm, a colonial house on a bluff overlooking the Cumberland River near Clarksville, Tennessee, where their daughter Nancy grew up. The farm and the life there — they had many visitors — were later to serve as background for *The Strange Children*. Here Caroline Gordon perfected her art, publishing a number of short stories and novels. Though few in number, the short stories gained for Miss Gordon her initial recognition, and she was awarded the second O. Henry Prize in 1934 for "Old Red." She did not collect her stories, however, until 1945 with *The Forest of the South* and 1963 with *Old Red and Other Stories*. The Tates were in Princeton from 1939 to 1942, and in Washington from September 1943 to June 1944 where Tate was poetry consultant at the Library of Congress.

Between 1946 and 1951 Miss Gordon lived partly in Sewanee, Tennessee, where Tate edited the *Sewanee Review*, and partly in Princeton where her daughter resides. During these years she taught a workshop in techniques of fiction at the Department of

General Studies, Columbia University; she has taught there several times since. In 1951, Tate went to the University of Minnesota; and the Tates lived in Minneapolis much of each year. Since the early 1950's, Miss Gordon has taught courses in fiction and creative writing at Minnesota colleges and at universities throughout the country.

A very important event in her life in the 1940's was her conversion to Roman Catholicism. Her celebration of an ordered past in her early fiction led her inevitably to explore the possibilities for an ordered present which Christianity extends to the believer. She has even been able to trace analogies between the writing of fiction and the practice of religion: both forms of the spiritual life require, she maintains, an imitation of "the patience of Christ" and a display of faith. For some time Miss Gordon has been working on *A Narrow Heart: The Portrait of a Woman*, a novel which she says will be her last.

The House of Fiction (1950; second edition, 1960) and *How to Read a Novel* (1957) are both invaluable for defining the kind of fiction which Miss Gordon writes. That she evolved her theory of fiction over a period of years is evident in her practice and in her pronouncements, which have come late. Ford, Flaubert, Chekhov, James, Crane, and Joyce, her admired forebears, confirmed her belief that fiction must embody a heightened psychological reality. As these writers did, she maintains that narrative art must be concerned with the conduct of life, especially with the relationships of people to one another and with the changes in these relationships. Aware of Aristotle and the example of Greek drama, the novelist will be sensitive to the "complications" arising among individuals which follow upon the "discovery" of crucial knowledge. Like the Greek dramatists, he next devotes his skill to the "resolving" of these complications, a process that depends upon the "peripety," the decisive change from one state to another.

In his analysis of personal relationships, the novelist must attempt to convey every nuance in the values and every shade in the feelings embodied in his characters. "A direct impression of life" will be the result, especially if he uses with a craftsman's skill the vivid detail and the vivid image to evoke his characters, their situations, and their emotions. In sum, the modern writer of fiction will control his energies in order to secure the greatest immediacy for the impressions he wishes to record. He will appreciate the resources provided by tone and style in attaining unity, precision, and consistency of effect. One characteristic of fiction since Hawthorne, Flaubert, and James, Miss Gordon asserts, has been the writer's recourse to vivid metaphors to render his vision; the more evocative of such metaphors function organically as symbols. The intensity of the artist's vision can also endow character, incident, and speech with more than ordinary import. So the artist will succeed to the extent that he gives his experience significance through the use of symbolically rich situations, characters, and images. So also, according to Miss Gordon, "the most characteristic literary trend of our time is a fusion of Naturalism and Symbolism."

With her study of James, Miss Gordon further refined her views on the technique of fiction. He it was who taught her the virtues of a restricted point of view and its importance for determining both form and spiritual authority in the novel. Nineteenth-century writers had made most frequent use of the "omniscient" or "panoramic" point of view which they alternated with a restricted or dramatized point of view when they focused on the individual scene. With Flaubert resort was had to a "concealed narrator" who interprets the action by inhabiting the minds of several characters, at the same time that he does not obtrude as spokesman for the author. It is therefore possible for the character to react directly to his experience as in a first-person narrative but to have these reactions interpreted implicitly by the author's superior intelligence which not only inhabits the character's consciousness but ranges above it.

The "central intelligence" that organizes a late James novel is an even more sophisticated interpreter of the action than is the concealed narrator. In this method the mind of one person constitutes an organizing medium as it develops his impressions, his evaluations of experience, and his growth in moral awareness. In this method we have the immediacy of the first-person mode, the flexibility of the omniscient mode, and the penetrativeness of the mode of the concealed narrator. The method of the central intelligence goes furthest in the dramatizing of the interior life.

As for Miss Gordon's own fiction, such a central intelligence operates at its purest in her two latest novels. In them the moral sensibilities of the leading characters organize the action as these protagonists reflect upon it and assimilate its implications. In her earlier books, Miss Gordon used the Flaubertian concealed narrator, since she did not confine the psychological drama to one person's mind. At the same time, she approached in them the method of the central intelligence because there is more exhaustive analysis of the mind of Catherine Chapman, for example, in *The Women on the Porch* than we find in novels not written in the Jamesean tradition. In any event, the main formal problem for Miss Gordon has been the securing of maximum "organic" authority for her presentation of life. This she has endeavored to achieve by an ever sharper demarcation, and an ever more sophisticated manipulation, of the mind which interprets the experiences dramatized in her novels.

Miss Gordon's use of symbolic naturalism is most clearly seen in her short stories. "The Brilliant Leaves," "The Presence," "Old Red," "Her Quaint Honour," "The Petrified Women," and "The Forest of the South" are some of her best and some of the best written in the present century. By their limited scope they have kept Miss Gordon confined to a single point of view. The short stories pre-eminently reveal her use of the vivid detail for establishing mood, for conveying subtleties of psychological shading, and for achieving the expansiveness of meaning that in literature we associate with symbolism.

Almost any of the stories illustrates Miss Gordon's method and accomplishment. "The Brilliant Leaves" is typical. It charts the disillusionment and frustration when ardent love disintegrates. The situation is complicated because the girl realizes that a change in the relationship has occurred while the boy does not. The superficiality of the boy's relatives in their neat houses; the disaster to his Aunt Sally when her father met her spineless lover with a shotgun; the brilliant, but soon to be decaying, leaves of autumn in contrast to the verdant glade in the woods to which the lovers retreat in order to recapture their passion; the beautiful waterfall there and the cliff that must be climbed to get the best view of it; the restive girl's impulse to climb the cliff and her falling to her death, whether by accident or by a subconscious drag toward death; the boy's panic and the girl's revulsion from him before her death — all comment implicitly upon the entanglements presented in the tale and give it a density of substance that eludes paraphrase.

Another story that treats realistically yet symbolically the contemporary scene is "Her Quaint Honour." Bud Asbury's lust for the Negro wife of a hired man leads to the spoiling of a fine tobacco crop for the first-person narrator who had hired Bud to supervise the firing. Not only do the characters and their conflicts embody the symbolism developed in the tale but so do nature and the agricultural life. Accordingly, the whole significance of the story is concentered in the image of the barn filled with prime tobacco, irreparably spoiled because the fires are damped as a result of Bud's irresponsibility and his yielding to momentary passion. And there is much irony in the narrator's having made his grandmother's fallow land blossom, only to witness the destruction of the wealth it produces because men do not love the land enough to work for it devotedly. More generally, the story points to the horror of a world in which lust takes the place of love and the cruelty of a caste system in which the Negro has few resources to withstand the depredations of a stronger race.

Some of the stories that are nearly contemporary in concern use Aleck Maury as first-person narrator or third-person controlling intelligence. His memoirs form the subject of *Aleck Maury Sportsman*; and all the Maury stories can be regarded as its spiritual appendages. "One More Time" and "The Last Day in the Field" follow the novel in using a first-person narrator. The former takes place in Florida where a friend of Maury's comes for one more fishing trip despite illness and an unsympathetic wife who little realizes that she has driven her husband to suicide. Nostalgic fervor pervades "The Last Day in the Field," as Maury, succumbing to age and failing physical powers, pays a ritual farewell to the chase that has sustained him for so long.

Excellent stories which use as method a central intelligence are "Old Red" and "The Presence." In "Old Red" Maury experiences some alienation from the members of his family, because they do not understand the frenetic nature of his devotion to sport. Social obligations and the conventions of society mean little to a man who is driven to compensate for the few years allotted him by his desire to fathom all the secrets of nature he can. Symbolically, Maury becomes the one who is persecuted by the conventions his relatives represent as he feels his own identity merge with that of "Old Red," the hunted fox. Just as "Old Red" barely escapes destruction by heroic effort, so Maury knows that, old as he is, he must struggle to the end against restrictive pressures. "The Presence" finds Maury in a mood of deep concern for others. Jim Mowbray is the best dog trainer and Jenny, Jim's wife, the best cook and kindest woman Maury has ever known. The loss is catastrophic to Aleck when Jim is unfaithful to Jenny; his friends have been more than friends, they have become symbols for him of a harmony rarely found among human beings. At seventy-five Maury finds that his stable world is about to dissolve and that he will again be homeless. He thinks of his orthodox Aunt Vic on her deathbed and his murmuring of the Angelic Salutation as a boy; he knows that he also needs the Holy Mary to pray for him at this moment which represents for him a spiritual death.

The stories dealing with the Civil War again illustrate Miss Gordon's recourse to symbolic naturalism as an artistic method. In these tales the situations and the details are realistic even while they convey a more than literal, an almost indefinable, intent. An individual image or metaphor often conveys the essence of a story, although other details elaborate further the significance of the work.

In "The Forest of the South" several such images coalesce to establish the impact of this tale: the madness of Mrs. Mazereau, the mistress of the Villa Rose plantation; the intensification of her daughter's disorders during the narrative; the Yankee killing, half by accident and half by design, of the returning Colonel Mazereau; the blowing up of the nearby estate, Clifton, because of a Yankee engineer's injured pride; the deserted Macrae mansion with its mute fountain as an emblem of lost greatness; the arrest there as a spy of Eugénie Mazereau's former lover by her Yankee fiancé, Lieutenant John Munford; the lover's subtle confirmation to Munford of Eugénie's insanity; and the comparison by Munford of Eugénie's eyelids to a magnolia blossom he had seen not long before: "When he had first come into the country he had gathered one of those creamy blossoms only to see it turn brown in his grasp." His love for Eugénie too will wither as the flower once did, for he proposes to her without knowing that she is mad. Once he knows, he is bound in honor to marry her, but he divines that his future with her will be torture for both of them. In this unpredictable world the conquered girl becomes the conqueror of her suitor; the madness of the invader's enterprise recoils on Munford when he innocently allies himself to a girl whose degeneration has been caused by those who have fought like himself for an ideal without being able to foresee the consequences of their actions. In "Hear the Nightingale Sing" a mentally unstable girl and a stubborn mule defeat a homeward-bound Yankee when he stifles his humane instincts and attempts to steal the mule, only to be thrown and killed by the animal's brute force. And a bizarre humor lightens the horror of "The Ice House" wherein two southern boys dig up Yankee skeletons for a federal contractor who fraudulently and haphazardly places the bones among the coffins he has brought with him. Such an entrepreneur is a favorite Agrarian symbol, the capitalist who without conscience pursues his own gain.

In *Penhally* (1931) Miss Gordon developed at still greater length the theme of the grandeur of the southern past compared to the diminished present. The novel has for central presence a place rather than a person; and Penhally, in its flourishing state before the Civil War and in its fall from power after the Reconstruction, is a symbol for the South, the antebellum way of life, and the attenuated survival of southern traditions into the present. In its heyday Penhally irradiated the security and the sense of purpose present in southern civilization before the war. Part I of the novel ends appropriately with some account of the Llewellyn men during the war. Penhally endures the depredations of war; and the stoic force of the house is inseparable from that of its owner, Nicholas Llewellyn.

As a psychological novel, *Penhally* dramatizes the division between Nicholas and his half-brother Ralph and the parallel conflict between Nick and Chance Llewellyn in the fourth generation of the family. Nicholas, traditional in point of view and tenacious of the land, believes in primogeniture and dispossesses Ralph. He is opposed to the war, for he regards land as a responsibility and does not want to participate in a venture that threatens his property. He does provide admirably for his dependents, including his slaves, during the war; and symbolically perhaps, he dies in 1866, when the South is conquered and Penhally's greatness is declining, though he is richer than at the war's beginning.

Ralph is improvident and less responsible than his brother in everyday affairs; and he lacks Nicholas' determination to hold his property at all costs. Yet there is much to admire in Ralph, since he despoils himself to support the Confederacy. Miss Gordon respects his devotion to principle, country, and heritage as much as she respects Nicholas' devotion to the soil. Ralph gives that his country may have life; Nicholas refuses to give so that he can keep life in the land. Some of the war sequences which end Part I are forceful — those concerned with the courtship by Charles Llewellyn of Alice Blair, his marriage to her, and his death as a cavalry officer. Other of these episodes relate loosely to the society and the characters presented in the novel and contribute little to its forward motion. Still, the impression registers that at no time was the South so great as in the hour of defeat.

Part II develops, at the Reconstruction, the first stage of the decline of Penhally and is the most moving section of the novel. John Llewellyn, who survived the war, inherits the estate but lacks the energy of his uncle Nicholas. Lassitude prevents him from functioning effectively, although he, too, loves the land and guards it jealously. His fatigue is matched by the instability of the cousin he marries, Lucy, the daughter of Ralph. She turns against John as a result of her misplaced energies and neurotic indisposition; but she survives into the 1920's as a twisted representative of tradition. The inability of John and Lucy to achieve a sympathetic relationship emphasizes the hopelessness of these years. The suicide of their son Frank, who had alienated Lucy by marrying a promiscuous cousin, adds to the oppressiveness of this part of the novel. Defeat in the war has been total, material and spiritual, local and national; and it goes beyond the conquered to infect the conquerors. John's decline is in part the result of inner debility, and this debility has its parallel in a nation weakened by a materialistic ethic. Thus John perceives "his own personal misfortunes monstrously shadowed in those of the nation."

In Part III Penhally remains, in the 1920's, a covert influence and a monument to a culture. The land has been entailed to Nick, grandson of John, although his brother Chance has the ancestral passion for the soil and Penhally house. Nick has, as it were, defected and uses his intelligence not to improve his inheritance but to establish himself in banking. The elder Nicholas splits in two in his twentieth-century descendants; Chance has his forebear's love of the farm and Nick his practical sense. Since Chance is a passionate man and since he is on the defensive about his values, he looms as a figure destined for involvement in tragic violence.

In the twentieth century harmonious human relationships are more possible than they were for the boys' grandparents, since war-induced trials of the spirit are now over. But in a deeper sense, a greater disunity prevails. Chance and Nick have strong affection for each other, yet Nick, because he has aligned himself with an aggressive materialism, is his brother's antagonist. The infection which had begun in Reconstruction has now reached the substratum of American life. Eastern millionaires overrun the region. Nick and his wife Phyllis cater to them; and he sells Penhally to Joan Parrish, who organizes a hunt club to take in the most fertile farms. The agrarian economy disintegrates as a new wealth, based on industrialism, takes over.

In general *Penhally* reveals little development in the characters and little intensification of conflict. The impressionistic technique, which allowed Miss Gordon to etch her characters brilliantly and to present individual scenes with much precision and evocativeness, led to excessive fragmentation as supernumerary personages and detachable incidents crowd the pages of the novel. It is in some respects, then, more tenuous than it ought to be. In certain others, it possesses an imaginative fullness that Miss Gordon was to control for notable results as her novels grew away from an episodic organization.

Aleck Maury Sportsman (1934) is Miss Gordon's only novel with a first-person narrator; and like *Penhally* it consists of a number of episodes arranged in linear time sequence. The elderly Maury recalls the main incidents of a life outwardly uneventful but for him rich with significance. Despite all pressures, especially the need to win worldly success and the demands of family upon him, Aleck Maury has had the strength of purpose to make his avocation — hunting and fishing — his vocation. Always he proceeds according to well-worked-out rituals and reads a sacramental significance into his ventures. His single-mindedness is epical in quality. Maury is a Ulysses figure, always seeking the new and untried, or an Aeneas figure, remaining constant to his aims through many wanderings. Reviewing his life since he was a boy, Maury realizes that he has brought all his resources of skill, caution, and patience to bear upon the chase and that he has succeeded as few men ever have. He has been as devoted to the techniques of sport as any true artist must be to the techniques of his calling. As a man of imagination himself, he pays tribute in "Old Red" to this quality in a friend of his by noting how rare it is: "He's a man of imagination. There ain't many in this world." His total involvement in his pursuits generates interest in the details of sporting lore that fill the novel and a nostalgic atmosphere as he recalls his ventures.

The quest is both inspiriting and sad. Whereas Maury attempts the impossible, the attempt gives him dignity. He knows that time will slip away and age overtake him before he has gone far in his explorations of nature. For a sportsman, as Maury says, "no day is ever long enough" and no effort is too great to make in the pursuit of his pleasures. In the sequences laid in Gloversville the tone is idyllic. The landscape induces an elation in Maury similar, he conjectures, to that known by the pioneers as they first came upon this country. The pool at West Fork sums up not only the joy he feels in nature but also his satisfaction with her, since the pool is all that a fisherman could ever hope to find.

The idyllic tone makes for a book in which the element of human conflict is muted. Except for his involvement with Molly, his wife, Maury's relationships with other people count for little. But he always regards his wife and children with the affection of a large-souled man, and he remains friendly with his associates unless they try to interfere with his vocation. Miss Gordon does exhibit much delicacy and subtlety in depicting Maury's life with Molly. In this instance, he is moved by the fate of someone external to himself. After his son drowns by accident, Maury divines that Molly thinks herself betrayed because he appears less grief-stricken than she does, and he is disturbed by this suggestion of division between them. If Maury's life is a personal search for the truth, the sincerity of his quest mitigates any hint of egotism in it. His dedication to some aspects of antebellum culture proves, moreover, that he is sensitive to ranges of value often disregarded in post-Civil War America.

The mood of the book is also elegiac. The "fatality tinged with sadness" which surrounds the death of Maury's Uncle James and the resignation implicit in the quoted last lines of *Oedipus Tyrannus* suffuse Maury's whole saga. Although he maintains that with "the halcyon days" at Gloversville and West Fork stream the melancholy of his childhood disappears forever, his very zest for life accentuates for him its evanescence. There are tragic aspects to Maury's career as well as rich fulfillments. The restless seeker learns that all aspiration is limited by the very nature of the human situation. The brutal aspects of nature are, upon occasion, disconcerting: see the quail that kill in his uncle's barn by tearing out each other's jugular veins. Some parts of life seem gratuitously senseless to Maury. The drowning of his son and the unlooked-for death of Molly are clouds on his existence almost impossible to dispel. Not only Dick's death but his birth had led to sober meditation instead of great joy: "I had never realized before with what reluctance a human soul faces this world." The autumnal sadness of age confers upon the pageantry of life as Maury has known it the bittersweet consistency of tone so prevalent in the book. The sustaining of this double-edged view of life as both exhilarating and poignant is the final measure of Miss Gordon's artistry in this novel.

In one segment of *The Garden of Adonis* (1937) Miss Gordon depicts agricultural life in the South, now devitalized as it was at the end of *Penhally* but containing within it sources for renewal if they can only be discovered by those who work the soil. The farm recession of the 1920's and the depression of the 1930's have caused much poverty; but men have also been careless of their agrarian heritage and have listened to the false gods of a mechanized culture. For all these reasons, a mode of existence which sustained men in the past can no longer do so.

The poverty of those who till the soil is equaled by the shiftlessness or the futility of their lives. Under the best circumstances the Sheelers would always have been failures. But even for admirable individuals life on the soil is rigorous, and rewards for the deserving Ote Mortimer and the conscientious Ben Allard are meager. Just as in *Penhally* affection ends in violence, so in this novel Ote turns upon his symbolic father, Ben. When Ben is unable to lend Ote money to marry the pregnant Idelle Sheeler and objects to his cutting the shared timothy and clover crop early, Ote in a fit of rage attacks with a single-tree from his mower the man who loves him. The assault presumably results in Ben's death, and demonstrates how even well-disposed individuals, motivated by affection and by passion for the earth, survive precariously, if at all, in a hostile age.

The passion and insight present in these scenes occur only fitfully in the other segment of the novel, the long middle section which devolves about Jim Carter and his frustrations. He derives from a genteel but poverty-stricken family; and like Ote and Ben, he is a victim. If anything, he has suffered more than they have from the defeat of aspiration. His rigorous, conventional mother has sacrificed him for her other children and has prevented him from following his bent as dog-trainer. He is defeated in his marriage to Sara Camp by a certain lack of imagination but also by her rootlessness and selfishness. And given his situation, his subsequent love for Ben's daughter, Letty, is hopeless. Jim and Sara are interesting characters, but Miss Gordon's analysis of them is sketchy. Nor do the members of Sara's family emerge clearly as individuals. They are rather her too patent subjects for satire as invading plutocrats, come to Alabama to exploit cheap labor.

The title indicates that Miss Gordon has made use of mythology to give her novel added ramifications of meaning. When the two strands of the story are viewed together, the epigraph of the novel, from Frazer's *The Golden Bough*, assumes a complex significance. The men are Adonis figures whose fates are determined, in part, by women who act irrationally when motivated by sexual passion: Sara disorganizes Jim, Idelle is false to Ote, and Letty betrays her father. Through myth Miss Gordon underlines her agrarian theme and bridges the two strands of her book. Ben Allard is a much less firm link between them. As a character he lacks centrality in the action and is convincing only as an ineffectual farmer and the victim of forces over which he has little control. In any case, the distinctive art that re-creates the lives and psychology of the poor white characters compensates for whatever impression we form of the novel as divided in structure and conception.

None Shall Look Back (1937) has the massive proportions associated with the epic; and in fact, Miss Gordon's model throughout seems to have been Tolstoi's epical *War and Peace*. Like Tolstoi she begins by presenting the aristocratic culture which war disrupts; and when war comes close, she adopts Tolstoi's technique of alternating panoramic battle scenes with nearer views of the main characters as they participate in the war or suffer behind the lines.

An epical hero, General Nathan Bedford Forrest, dominates activity in the field much as General Kutuzov does in Tolstoi's book. At all times, Forrest is the commanding presence in Miss Gordon's book from the time he is seen worrying about supplies

21

in the early days of the conflict until his last days on the field as still a formidable antagonist in the months of southern defeat. When Rives Allard, the fictional hero and one of Forrest's scouts, retires from action because of a wound, Miss Gordon takes advantage of his absence to enter Forrest's mind directly and to record one of the chief battles through his consciousness. Largely because he is seen so completely from within and without, he is not only a great historical figure but a novelistic character who appeals with aesthetic authority to our emotions and imaginations. In short, we are involved in the drama of his life. We identify with him when he opposes Generals Pillow and Floyd who counsel the disastrous surrender of Fort Donelson; when he engages in angry parley at Chickamauga with the indecisive Bragg; when he holds his dying brother in his arms at Okolona; and when, at Franklin, thinking of the deaths of his brother and General Cleburne, he perceives that death had always been at his side and he now understands, without endorsing it, the prudence of his superiors who had wanted to keep death at a distance. Like Kutuzov, Forrest possesses the preternatural insight which gives him greatness. Like the Russian, Forrest intuitively appraises a situation which neither he nor any other man can clearly define. Unlike Kutuzov, Forrest is sometimes ineffective because his intuitions are countermanded by his superiors who can only proceed according to rule and who are always cautious, never bold.

Some of the battle scenes are not organically part of the novel and reveal the weakness of the panoramic method. When Miss Gordon uses the Flaubertian concealed narrator and records action or psychology through the minds of her central characters, she much more successfully creates a universe possessing imaginative immediacy. Principally, she views the action through the eyes of Rives Allard and of Lucy Churchill, successively distant relative, sweetheart, wartime wife, and, finally, widow of Rives. Occasionally, some of the other characters reflect the action and their emotions, since Miss Gordon's extended canvas requires a roving narrator. Sometimes she even enters the minds of military figures who are peripheral to the main line of the novel. Still the impression remains that this is the story of Rives Allard and Lucy Churchill and, at another level, that of General Forrest.

Throughout, Miss Gordon contrasts the assertive forces of life, which also informed the gracious antebellum culture, with the negative forces of death and destruction as they overwhelm, with Götterdämmerung finality, this culture and its advocates. The woman Lucy is seen as the life-affirming individual, while the warrior Rives becomes aligned in part with the destructive forces that he struggles against. Man, the pioneer and protector of the hearth, is juxtaposed with woman who renews the life of the race and elaborates the arts of peace. The warrior who protects has no protection himself. This Lucy realizes when a skirmish is fought outside the home of the Georgia Allards and a Confederate captain is brought inside to die. Lucy now perceives that Rives, being human, may also die, and she can hardly bear the weight of this knowledge.

The two most powerful scenes in the novel dramatize the confrontation between the powers of life and death as they may be associated with Lucy and Rives respectively. On the field at Chickamauga, not far from his home, Rives searches through the multitude of the dead to find the body of his school friend George Rowan. After a sickening search Rives finds George's body and buries it. On such a battlefield as this, the mop-up is a gruesome process from which even seasoned soldiers recoil; and Rives reacts with the same fascinated horror that suffuses Hemingway's nightmarish "Natural History of the Dead." It is here that Rives, a potentially dead man among the dead, fortuitously meets Lucy who walks among the dead and dying, asserting by her very presence a defiance of the death which surrounds her on every side. Lucy is helping Rives's mother, who has engineered a volunteer operation to remove the wounded men from the field to an improvised hospital in the closest home and grove of trees. Amid this desolating scene, Rives responds to Lucy's presence and is able to withdraw from his preoccupation with war and death to the point of loving his wife in the few moments they can snatch from war and caring for the wounded.

The second sequence occurs near the end of the novel when Rives is on leave in Georgia to recover from a wound. Lucy is unprepared for his gradual withdrawal from her, as though he has business elsewhere which does not involve her. The lines and hollows of his face and its deathlike pall oppress her as she gazes at the sleeping man beside her. His brutal talk in his sleep horrifies her, and she recalls with involuntary revulsion that her husband is, actually, a spy. She hardly recognizes the man she loves, and she can hardly endure the changes that war has caused in him. Something more central than domestic life or love of woman has laid hold of him; war and imminent death make the purely personal gratifications seem irrelevant. The dance which Susan Allard arranges, with depleted resources, is a melancholy rather than a joyous affair. It becomes, in effect, a ritual farewell to the soldiers about to leave for the field, a preliminary dance of death in parallel sequence to the dance at the Rowans' early in the novel when the soldiers first go off to war. Then the dance was an expression of expectant triumph and a life-inciting rite, a fertility ritual.

The incompetence of the Confederate generals in the West increases the fatality which pervades the central characters and their land. The ability and discernment of the generals are incommensurate with the moral and spiritual qualities of the people they are defending. Death is associated with the Confederate cause from the time those in command fail to exploit their victories. The generals lack both the absolute selflessness and the realistic insight that would have brought victory. Only the subordinate generals Hill and Forrest possessed both ranges of qualities. Even Lee, dedicated as he was, lacked the realism that might have saved the situation in the West; and Jefferson Davis was foolishly loyal to all those to whom he had once entrusted power. Part of the trouble with the South, too, was the very fervor of its idealism. Thus George Rowan, like Lucy, feels revulsion at Rives for being a spy. Yet without accurate intelligence of Federal movements, Forrest could not have achieved his victories; and part of Bragg's failure was his inability to use information once he was supplied with it.

War not only produces actual death but death-in-life as well. War brutalizes a good man, when Rives, for example, becomes proficient in the conscript guard. War makes an old man of Ned Allard after his three years at Johnson's Island prison camp: a man from whom all energy has gone, a man whose eye seems no longer to see. Fontaine Allard, whose birthday celebration opens the book on an idyllic note, is unable to recover from the burning of his house and the despoiling of his property. Not only the great house goes, but so does the original structure of the first cabin which is outlined in the flames before the whole structure collapses. War burns and destroys, then, to the very roots of a culture. And death sears the living. With Rives's death, Lucy knows that she will see the Kentucky landscape in an alien light. But the fact that she can think at all of "the green fields of Kentucky" argues for something indestructible in Lucy, in the human spirit itself.

The artistry of the novel resides in Miss Gordon's skilled intertwining of her central characters with the fortunes of the South.

As individuals involved in the basic experiences of love, war, and death Rives, Lucy, and General Forrest are capacious enough to objectify Miss Gordon's mythic vision. Their emotions and conflicts stretch beyond their immediate situations and attain a significance that is universal. In a very real sense, then, her characters speak for all human beings who become involved in a cataclysmic war.

In the image of the westward road on the first page of *Green Centuries* (1941) and its attractiveness for Rion Outlaw, the protagonist, there is established a central motive of this novel which portrays the life of southern colonials as they push beyond the Blue Ridge. Always, however, practical necessity tempers romantic impulse. Rion Outlaw would like to go with Daniel Boone in the early pages of the book, but he cannot afford a horse. Later, he does not go beyond the Watauga region in western North Carolina though fabulous Kentucky lures him and Boone again invites him to go. If Rion feels the wilderness call him, he is aware that he is settling a family on the frontier and cannot abandon his responsibilities as citizen, husband, and father.

Rion is a complex person who wishes to subdue the wilderness to the order of civilization at the same time that the innovative spirit of the pioneer calls him away from a settled existence. He is the romantic who eternally seeks and who is perpetually disappointed. He is to some degree a spiritual outlaw, regarding himself as beyond the ordinary constraints laid upon mankind, and he resists the advent of law in the new community. Rather, he works in accord with the basic laws of his own being which enable him at times to achieve notable, if inadequate, results. If Rion is complacent about his own powers, he is industrious and draws satisfaction from his wife Cassy, the land he cultivates, and his children. In 1776, at the end of five years in the wilderness, he has a farm of twenty acres and feels just pride in the fruits of his labors. His devotion to the land, in fact, anticipates the rapport that men felt for it, according to Miss Gordon, in the antebellum civilization of the South. His most reprehensible aspect is a willingness to regard the Indians as subhuman. And the hatred with which he fights them after Cassy leaves him to visit a sick neighbor brings its own nemesis, as he unknowingly shoots his brother and his Indian wife on land that the Indians have recently settled.

Rion and Cassy are the victims of forces that reach beyond them. External catastrophe and the inability of the psyche to withstand great shock defeat them. There is nothing dishonorable in Rion's aligning himself with the Regulators and his rebellion against British tyranny. But after defying British soldiers, he flees his native region for the frontier to escape being hanged. Then as settler in a new land, there is nothing dishonorable in his alliance with those who stand against British authority. The view that Rion is the prideful, self-sufficient, godless man, and as such typical of the pioneers, is true to a point. But it is this outlaw element that also gives him decisiveness and creative force.

Cassy Dawson becomes the selfless wife and mother, and has more power than Rion to analyze her situation. Her introspective temperament is sometimes a liability as it fosters an undue sense of alienation. She is happy for five years with Rion on the Holston; but, when the two oldest children are scalped, she succumbs to morbid guilt. In her misery she refuses the only anodyne, her husband's devotion which is sexual as well as spiritual. In recoil from him, she drives him to the infidelity which only intensifies her bitterness and brings her to neurotic collapse. Earlier, she had loved Rion for himself more than for the security he could give her. Even after the death of her children she thinks first of her husband and not of herself as she counsels him to cry no more. But soon her self-command vanishes, and her own gaze turns inward and destroys her. In the last sequences she withholds love and irrationally expects Rion's feeling for her to remain the same. At Cassy's death both Rion and Cassy are apologetic, and each confesses the wrong done the other. In essence, each has in life's journey turned aside from the true way of mutual affection.

Miss Gordon throughout stresses the difficulties in establishing order in a strange environment. Simply, they are often too great to be borne. This truth reaches Rion when in his concluding reverie he thinks of the significance of his name and now learns the cost in human terms of the westward venture: "Did Orion will any longer the westward chase? No more than himself. Like the mighty hunter he had lost himself in the turning. Before him lay the empty west, behind him the loved things of which he was made. . . . Were not men raised into the westward turning stars only after they had destroyed themselves?"

Ironically, one form of order, that represented by the culture of the Indians, is fated to disappear. Although he is in a vital relationship to nature, the Indian is not able to adjust to alien modes of social existence and the white man's callousness. The Indians have values and rituals which unite them into an organic society; and they possess a poise and serenity often absent from the white man. But they are cruel and vindictive and reveal few compunctions in their treatment of captives. Miss Gordon appreciates the stamina and courage of the Indian, but does not regard him as a moral exemplar. She is skeptical of the noble-savage view and knows that European civilization brings possibilities for ranges of insight and order unknown to the Indian. At the same time it brings disease, firearms, and unsuspected depths of perfidy.

In the main characters we have the partial failure of qualities which sustained the characters in *None Shall Look Back*. The failure of creative masculinity and conservative feminism to keep intact a harmonious existence under frontier conditions is one chief theme in *Green Centuries*. Miss Gordon's increased emphasis on human limitation would argue that she was now moving toward a Christian orientation. From the beginning she had recognized candor and generosity as essential qualities in human relationships; what she began to recognize now was the precariousness of such relationships in the absence of a divine sanction.

In the green woods of America at any rate, Eden cannot be recaptured, at best only glimpsed. The paradisal wilderness is only superficially a paradise and more truly a wilderness as the epigraph, by John Peale Bishop, would indicate: "The long man strode apart./ In green no soul was found,/ In that green savage clime/ Such ignorance of time." Rion's observing the swans that tear each other apart persuades him and us of the brutality of nature; the brutality of men is implicit in another image, of Negroes being taken westward and chained together in the straw of covered wagons as if they were chattel goods.

One of the virtues of the novel resides in the characters who are complex without being sophisticated. This complexity and their basic reality make them timeless. The novel also extends toward universality because of Miss Gordon's recourse to myth; thereby the personae achieve added dimensions without themselves having to articulate them. So Rion learns from the Apollo figure (Cassy's brother, Frank) that he has been named for the Greek giant and hunter Orion. Rion possesses the grandeur and strength, some of the moral force, too, associated with a god, something, moreover, of the restlessness of the prototypic hunter. Cassy as a Diana figure (in the legend she kills Orion by accident) has at first the stature of a goddess, and then loses authority as she succumbs to morbid thoughts. The name Cassy suggests affinity with the pathetic and forsaken Cassandra, a woman unfairly overcome by fate. Cassy's formal name, Jocasta, recalls to us the heroine of the Oedipus legends whose end was as tragic as it was unexpected.

In many ways *Green Centuries* is an expressive novel, successful within the limitations Miss Gordon imposed on herself. Her style is careful and exact, her ear for speech is unerring, and her eye for the precise detail is sure. The novel builds impact slowly and is more powerful in retrospect than as we read it first. The middle sections go on at too great length; and Archy Outlaw lacks force and development for a crucial character. As a result he cannot sustain interest in the chapters depicting the culture of the Indians. The earlier chapters are excellent, particularly as they describe the troubled love between Rion and Cassy and his involvement with the Regulators. But the best sequences are those at the end which treat the growing rift between Rion and Cassy. As the tenderly built harmony of their lives is destroyed, we become aware that time and process erode even the most conscientious and loving relationships.

The Women on the Porch (1944) is the last of Miss Gordon's books in her earlier manner and the first of her books in her later manner. The technique is that of the Flaubertian narrator, in which the author enters the minds of many people. A more explicit use of the Joycean stream of consciousness prevails here than in her preceding books; and these explorations into the unconscious possess much lyrical intensity. Many of the details have symbolical value: as in *The Garden of Adonis* and *Green Centuries*, mythology enlarges the meaning of character and incident.

The central drama concerns Catherine Chapman, scion of a decaying family of Tennessee aristocrats, and her husband Jim, a history professor in New York. He is unfaithful to Catherine, inexplicably even to himself, after several years of placid marriage. As in *Green Centuries*, Miss Gordon knows the difficulty of maintaining human relationships in a world in which meaningful values exist precariously. The city, for example, is a kind of queen bee in wild flight which leads all her inhabitants to destruction so long as they remain passive, careless, and uncritical in their personal lives.

Both Catherine and Jim must experience hell and be rescued therefrom before they appreciate each other. New York is hell, an inferno, wherein values that ought to be esteemed are lightly discounted. Jim has lost the dedication that led him to compose a history of Venice; and he gets no sustenance from friends, less even from Edith Ross, the superficial intellectual who becomes his mistress. He realizes his loss only after Catherine has been gone a few weeks; by the time he leaves in pursuit of her, the intensity of his feeling reminds us of Orpheus' plaints for Eurydice in the early scenes of *Orfeo ed Euridice*. In a letter to me Miss Gordon states that when she was writing this novel, "I was haunted by Gluck's opera . . . Both by the music and by his version of the Orpheus story . . . it was chiefly the form of the opera which impressed me. At any rate, I was conscious of parallels between the form of the opera and that of my novel."

Jim has never identified himself with any thing, person, or place: "I do not belong anywhere. There is no place anywhere that is a part of me." In his relationship with Catherine he had known a steadiness and strength that nothing else has ever given him. The portrait in the Chapman apartment of Catherine caressing a unicorn hints at her unusual nature, her purity (the unicorn is a symbol of chastity), and her reserves of spirit. Jim's reading Dante emphasizes the inferno-like nature of his surroundings and brings him to a new awareness, for he perceives that he has indeed departed from "the straight way" "in the middle" of his life. He perceives, moreover, that sexual intimacy gives knowledge of another person impossible to come by in any other way: "Did the woman who once truly received a man become the repository of his real being and thenceforward, witch-like, carry it with her wherever she went?" He has never before realized the sanctity of marriage as a relationship built on sex but going far beyond it.

Catherine has gone to her family homestead, Swan Quarter, hoping to find, in tradition and in proximity to the land, values that will steady her. Since the death of her Uncle Jack in a fall from a horse, Swan Quarter has been the home of three elderly relatives who remind us of the Fates or Norns. As frustrated and barren women, they are the presiding powers at her journey's end. In poignant sequences Catherine's grandmother and Aunt Daphne Passavant relive their tragedies. Catherine Fearson remembers the anguish of the war and her lover's wound; he lost the power of speech and lived apart from others while Catherine, feeling she may have betrayed him, married his brother. Aunt Daphne recalls how her lover had jilted her on her honeymoon night; a friend of hers had arranged this match as a joke, leading the man to think that Daphne had a fortune. The admirable Aunt Willy Lewis has learned to live without delight and refuses love simply because she has become accustomed to doing without it.

Instead of being a refuge for Catherine, Swan Quarter becomes a more disheartening hell than the city had been. Like Eurydice, Catherine will be rescued by a determined mate who has learned her true worth. The atmosphere in these sequences is close to that of Gluck's opera. Most often house and grounds are seen at night or in an autumnal setting. For Catherine, the house contains ghostly presences which seem to prophesy evil and force her into Tom Manigault's company the night after Aunt Willy leaves for the fair to exhibit Red, her fine stallion. Close to the end, Jim comes from New York through a desolate September landscape; he arrives at dusk, feels his passion for Catherine revive, and knows uncontrollable jealousy when Catherine confesses to an affair with Tom. As the shadows lengthen, like an infuriated Othello he virtually strangles her and is only saved by her insistence that he cease. While Jim's fingers had been about his wife's neck, he had seemed to look into an abyss; and this abyss still yawns before him until his reconciliation with her. Husband and wife prepare for a new life after the terrors of this long night. They decide to leave just as light is about to scatter the darkness and the shadows clouding their souls. Aunt Willy's homecoming with her report of Red's accidental electrocution hastens their departure. In Red's death we see that the unassisted life energies are not so strong as they appear to be; their power is limited, and they fail to provide in themselves any durable basis, moral or metaphysical, for existence.

Catherine is not only a Eurydice figure, but like Cassy Outlaw she brings to mind such other forsaken women in legend as Ariadne or Iphigenia; in her patient overcoming of suffering she is like Saint Catherine, her namesake; and she seems also a Persephone figure who has retreated for a season into Hades. Jim brings Catherine out of hell away from the darkness of decaying Swan Quarter; yet in some sense Catherine also rescues him from his own spiritual hell. Her dream of a dead man's spirit for whose safety she is responsible would seem to indicate that she stands in this vital relationship to Jim. As in Gluck's opera, the characters experience both the pangs and the delights, and then the transcendent power, of love. Jim and Catherine now know the truth that their mythological prototypes learned before them, that the claims of love are overpowering and cannot be lightly foregone: "For Love's every captive humbly rejoices;/ None would go free that ever wore his chain!"

The Strange Children (1951) presents through the central intelligence of the nine-year-old Lucy Lewis a view of the adult world which surrounds her as she attempts to relate herself to it. The most remarkable facet of the novel is the consistency with which Miss Gordon maintains point of view and the thoroughness with which she charts the development in Lucy of moral and religious awareness. Kevin Reardon, a visiting friend of the family, explains that she is named after Saint Lucy whose name means light: one so named should be able to experience an accession of light as Lucy in fact does.

Miss Gordon depicts with subtlety the tensions between Lucy and the adults about her, "the strange children" of the title "whose mouth speaketh vanity." If Lucy is a "changeling" to her mother, Sarah Lewis is, for the girl, an object of pity as she drudges for the guests, of bewilderment as she suffers from a hangover, and of antagonism as she tries to prevent Lucy from going with Uncle Tubby and Isabel Reardon for a swim. Tubby MacCollum is a "successful" poet whose work about the Civil War, *If It Takes All Summer*, has been immensely popular; he has visited the Reardons in France recently, and Isabel has telegraphed him to meet her at the Lewises'. Stephen Lewis, Lucy's father, is a lapsed poet and an amateur historian, too intellectual to be capable of spontaneity. Lucy notes her parents' tendency to disparage their friends; and in her mind's eye, she sees the dismembered bodies of these people lying about the lawn when her parents are done with their gossiping.

Throughout, Lucy thus modulates her sensations and thoughts from the conscious plane to the unconscious, passing from articulate utterance to the half-formed impressions and the psychic fluctuations of the stream of consciousness. In addition, she frequently juxtaposes the perceptions of the moment with dim recollections of her past in France and elsewhere. She is shaken by the discovery of Tubby and Isabel embracing in the woods, intuitively understanding what is happening though she is unable to define her reactions precisely. Evil thus disturbs her before she knows enough about it to come to terms with it.

Lucy Lewis continually learns about her elders and is able to use some of this knowledge for her own enlightenment. Her own imaginativeness and spontaneity are symbolized through her involvement with the characters in the romantic tale of *Undine* which she constantly ponders. And like Undine, Lucy acquires a soul and learns of both the sufferings and the satisfactions which knowledge brings. She regards the world of pretentious intellectuals with the asperity of Aleck Maury, her grandfather; the old man regards his daughter, her husband, and their friends as fools who bore him. Lucy would agree with her grandfather that unspoiled nature is more vital than the "civilized" life of her parents and their circle. She experiences a peace in contemplating the waterfall, for instance, which she finds nowhere else at Benfolly.

Lucy illustrates in her own actions the basic truth that evil impulses divide human nature. She cannot retain an unsoiled virtue in the decadence that surrounds her. She steals a crucifix from Reardon. When she returns it, she confesses her theft in a kind of penance rite. The eyes of the crucifix have fascinated her, and they will undoubtedly have a renovative effect upon her in the future. She finds the same depths of understanding in Reardon's eyes, and she feels especial remorse at her theft when she learns that he is buying her a pony. The eyes of the crucifix and Reardon's awaken in her a sense of moral perspective, but she is reluctant to face the implications of inner change. But Reardon's spiritual presence is so compelling that she cannot evade the man who acts upon her like a "hound of heaven."

Lucy has gotten further in moral enlargement than most of the other characters have. But in the last two pages, light breaks into the soul of Stephen Lewis and the point of view shifts to him. Born under Scorpio he realizes now the true meaning of this zodiacal sign, "The House of Death — unless a man be reborn." He sees that he and all men have desert places to cross and that life is a pilgrimage involving both a progression and an unknown goal. Stephen at last surmounts his intellectual pretensions and his arid way of discounting spiritual experience.

No longer will he be able to do as he had done when he belittled Reardon's vision of the saint who succored him after an accident in France. Sarah had been impressed with Reardon's recital and had complained of her husband's callow comments upon it. She asserts, in fact, that Stephen's intellect inhibits his feelings and prevents them both from being able to grasp life's ineffable dimensions. But at the end Stephen is ready to admit that transcendental values may exist.

The coda at the end is in sequence with an earlier high point when Lucy in a dream had seen all the Benfolly adults now journeying through a dark wood; her father and mother separate to go each his own way. From another path comes Isabel carrying a trencher with a man's head on it, that of a Captain Green murdered by his personal servant in the Civil War. Isabel scares away her husband and Tubby, her admirer; and we have intimations that she is a sinister person. The people are traversing not a forest but a wasteland on the edge of a chasm; and they can only be saved from death by turning back to the arduous path they had come by. Lucy thus sees modern man as both a victim of spiritual paralysis and a wanderer in a wasteland; her perceptions are essentially those of Stephen when he views his own plight and that of his family and friends. The visions are so closely connected that the modulation in point of view in the last two paragraphs from Lucy's to Stephen's represents no violation of aesthetic probability.

In *The Strange Children*, Miss Gordon is fascinated with the subject of religion. Lucy represents the receptive mind, the person who has not lost the ability to feel. Unless one becomes as a little child, Miss Gordon implies, he will never be able to see God. Stephen Lewis and his friend Tubby are agnostics by intellectual preference, temperamental dryness, and excessive pride; Sarah Lewis' Uncle Fill voices a militant, unsophisticated skepticism. Sarah possesses the religious temperament without religious conviction; the Holy Rollers, who hold their meetings on the Lewis farm, possess religious conviction but are wayward, extreme, and mindless. Kevin Reardon is a Roman Catholic and a source of truth. As a result of his accident, his vision then, and his devotion to his wife, he has achieved humility, grace, and religious knowledge. He had, as a young man, spurned the religious devotions of his father; his conversion is one way whereby he makes peace with a parent he had only seen that one time since childhood. Reardon in acknowledging his Heavenly Father has acknowledged his earthly father as well. Reardon is distressed by the irreligion of his friends, particularly as that reaches sacrilege when, in charades, Tubby impersonates a priest, acting out the name Parnell, which, according to Tubby, means "priest's mistress." The Lewises perceive finally that their patronizing judgments of Reardon as drifter and religious pretender are mistaken. The madness of his wife also seems to mirror the madness of a world that does not appreciate Reardon's values.

Madness in Isabel is paralleled by the frenzy let loose in the meeting of the Holy Rollers. They follow the teachings of Arnold Watkins whom God had commanded to follow the text "They shall take up serpents; and if they drink any deadly thing, it shall not hurt them." So they tempt providence by charming rattlesnakes; as a result, Terence MacDonough, Lewis's tenant, is bitten and barely escapes death. A more genuine faith than theirs can actually subdue savage beasts. Thus Saint Marthe tamed a wild dragon with her girdle; and Reardon, born on her day, has lived to subdue the beast in himself through a life of discipline which neither the evangelical Rollers nor his agnostic associates attain.

The conflicts of the characters within the self and with each other are genuine; in retrospect the situations the people are in, their spiritual dilemmas, interest us most. The tone is, if anything, neutral and understated, and the characters are seen with perhaps excessive objectivity. For Miss Gordon's characters, heroic action is not quite possible. As for her one heroic person, Reardon, we do not see the truth about him soon enough for the novel to center upon him as well as upon Lucy Lewis. In *The Malefactors* (1956), Miss Gordon solved this problem by making Catherine Pollard spiritually central to the novel from the first time she appears in it, even though the skeptical poet Tom Claiborne is the central intelligence.

Claiborne is, like Stephen Lewis, a lapsed middle-aged poet, who has lost the capacity to relate freshly to life. He is restless and sensitive, because his creativity is thwarted. Vera, his wife, makes his life an easy but a barren one on her Pennsylvania estate. One of his shallow associates describes, in a moment of insight, Claiborne's failing, his never having "been aware of the existence of another human being." When he and Vera separate over his affair with her cousin Cynthia Vail, he attacks Vera in order to defend himself, accusing her of his own preoccupation with the self. Claiborne later sees the truth, how he has described a circle about himself and struck away any living things springing up in it. How then, he wonders, can he now expect Vera to breathe willingly "the impoverished air" which envelops him?

Claiborne is a misguided son of the world instead of a son of light. His secular values extinguish the poetic inspiration which had once been genuine; and the "cold determination to write more verses" which followed upon his early creativity has been stultifying. With creativity gone and nothing left to arouse him to loyalty or action, it is not surprising that he envies Keats his early death. Nor is it surprising, once the prop of marriage is gone, that Vera tries to gain release from her empty life through suicide. When his affair with Cynthia goes flat, Claiborne realizes that Vera had been searching for darkness and that he, too, has been seeking such oblivion all his life. The death wish grows powerful, then, as he contemplates jumping from his apartment house window.

Miss Gordon's notable achievement is to keep us interested in the culpable Claiborne. We are immediately immersed in his situation and in his evaluations of his contemporaries and his own past life. They are often perceptive, for he knows the weaknesses of the people in his set; and he can see clearly, within limits, his own acts. He has intelligence and talent in desuetude to offset his failures in sympathy, imagination, and purposiveness. The fact, too, that he can learn from experience elevates him over most of the other people in the novel who are satisfied with life in a secular and hedonistic wasteland. His associates are the malefactors, so named because they do wrong and recall the criminals crucified with Christ, one of whom resisted salvation even while he was dying. Claiborne at least retains the poet's receptivity toward experience even if he has lost the power to interpret it meaningfully.

Before long he perceives the worth of Vera whom he has abandoned for life with the literary Cynthia. Cynthia has green, vixen-like eyes in contrast to Vera's blue, steady gaze. Cynthia's beauty and talent blind him to her shallow, calculating nature; and it is not until after they give a large party that he sees her for what she is, a self-centered person even more guilty than he has been of a failure to "know how other people feel." As for

Vera, we at first see her through Claiborne's eyes and judge her with his good-natured indulgence and latent dissatisfaction. Her activities as a lady farmer do not channel her energies effectively and, in fact, make her seem faintly ridiculous. Her involvement with Bud, the prize Red Poll bull, reveals a connoisseur's fussiness more than the Christian's love for a form of created life. The fete which she stages in honor of the bull is in part a thanksgiving rite, in part a Saturnalia; and the bull itself suggests a priapic deity. The bull is not only a sexual but a reality symbol. After the party is over, Claiborne feels there is more truth in the bull's vitality than he or his friends will ever express. The revulsion with which both Claiborne and Vera receive the propaganda of the inseminator at the fete reveals them both as opposed to the coarser manifestations of a secular culture. They regard this man's manipulations of nature as unnatural and contrary to the way that things were meant to be.

Gradually, Vera's strengths emerge. Her love for Claiborne is unquestioned if too protective. For one thing, she wants him to return to her after he has begun the affair with Cynthia; for another, she knows such excess of feeling that she attempts suicide. When her latent Catholicism awakes, however, she finds completion in tending Joseph Tardieu (the now senile author of *The Green Revolution*) and a physically deprived little boy, while she works on one of Catherine Pollard's farms. Claiborne accuses her of interested motives in not granting him a divorce so that she can more readily retain the child.

But he sees how baseless this accusation is when he looks directly into her blue eyes. Hitherto he had evaded her glance because it made him uncomfortable; her innocence was an affront, and he hated her momentarily because of her scrutiny of his face when she found him in Cynthia's apartment. Her eyes "are the mirror of the soul" and symbolize the spiritual realities basic to her nature, though her life with Claiborne for a while over-shadows them; and her eyes have an intensity comparable in their effects to Beatrice's in *The Divine Comedy*. Claiborne also over-comes his aversion to his dead father especially after a friend, the psychiatrist George Crenfew, interprets one of his dreams. George explains how, in the dream, the elder Claiborne had tried to pro-tect his son from the excesses of his nature, especially the tendency to blunt his emotions by intellectualizing his experiences. The epigraph from Maritain, "It is for Adam to interpret the voices that Eve hears," comments upon Claiborne's failure until the end to bring his mind into a fruitful relationship with intuition.

In his course toward enlightenment, two Roman Catholics help him. Sister Immaculata is writing a study of the dead homo-sexual poet Horne Watts, who had been a friend of the Clai-bornes in their expatriate years and who gains some of his force through his resemblances to Hart Crane. She instructs Claiborne that the heart of man is wicked but that no man need yield to all his impulses. There is hope, too, for fallen man, since "the Humanity of the Word," as Watts perceived, is the bridge be-tween earth and heaven. She regards God as the Hound of Heaven who tracks us down when we would avoid him. Claiborne is im-pressed by her in spite of his agnosticism.

Catherine Pollard is modeled in part on Dorothy Day, a Catho-lic well known for her philanthropy in the 1930's and later in behalf of New York City outcasts. Catherine is the other agent in Claiborne's renovation, a beautiful woman who has turned from a frivolous life to saintlike effacement. She now runs a shelter in New York and some farms in outlying regions for the homeless. For her these outcasts are not "offal" but "Christ," and "we must be Christ to them." For all his skepticism, Clai-borne recognizes unusual sensations in Catherine's presence: ease and a sense of relaxation, a sense of being plunged into an unknown element, a sense that he and she may be going toward a common goal. She also asserts that Horne Watts, through all the disorders of his life, was trying to find love, that "the love of love" sustained him through his sufferings. In Claiborne's last dream, Horne Watts guides him to a praying woman who resembles Catherine before she fades from sight. This is a sign to him that he should seek her out in his own extremity; and he finds her in Saint Eustace's chapel adjoining her shelter. She encourages him to seek Vera again although Vera has just rejected his overtures. Vera is a Catholic, Catherine asserts, and recognizes the sacramental aspect of marriage and will be subject to her husband as the Church is subject to Christ. Through Catherine, Claiborne learns that human relationships must be cherished and made firm through love, and he discovers the authority of a spiritual reality that transcends the self.

The book abounds in Christian images, particularly those connected with the saints featured in it, Catherine of Siena, Saint Ciannic whose statue is in the Claiborne garden, and Saint Eustace. The latter's miraculous powers and ultimate failure indicate that the Christian faith can move mountains and yet be ineffectual in many worldly contingencies. Eustace was a Roman general converted to Christianity when he saw the sign of the Cross poised between the horns of a deer. He and his family tamed the lions to which they were exposed but succumbed when they were thrust into a brazen bull and burned to death. Insofar as Bud's animalism is destructive, he may be linked with the bull in the Eustace legend or with the minotaur figure of the classics. The fete in honor of the bull at Vera's farm takes place in 1946 on the feast day of Saint Eustace, September 22. This has been through no design on Vera's part, despite her own fondness for the saint, at least for his church in Rome.

Most effective in extending the perspectives of the book are

Claiborne's dreams. These primarily concern caves and have some basis in his experience. He had explored much in caves when a boy. In a cave similar to one which he and George had found long ago, he and Cynthia have their first carnal contact. Claiborne's recurring dream is of a broad river that opens into a cavern. In the dream the current swirls him along until he sees the cavern yawning for him at the end of a tributary stream. The dream always ends here until the affair with Cynthia gains momentum. Then he is swept into the cavern itself. The cavern represents the chaos and the flux of the unconscious life, which can be terrifying without some clue how one is to travel through it. He wishes to begin a new life with Cynthia, even if this means consulting like Saul the Witch of Endor or descending like Odysseus to Orcus to gain intelligence from the dead. In Cynthia's company he seems to be wandering in a vast cavern while she casts a new (but not necessarily valid) light on the figures of all the people he has known. In another dream a woman guards the stairs leading to a vast hall below. Once there, he sits at a table with others, only to find that their robes cover figures without flesh; and he knows then that he is in hell. In Cynthia's presence, we can infer, he sees things falsely and he yields to dark, mindless, corrosive, evil instincts. She is no reliable guide in exploring the deepest facets of the self, although at first he experiences with her a release of powers that have long been submerged within him.

The caves of the unconscious may illuminate as well as obscure; and they allow us to confront, for what they are, the elemental realities of the self. In a dream that has for locale the cave that he and George once found, his father prevents him from throwing himself over a cliff and destroying himself as Horne Watts and Carlo Vincent (the mad painter who was Vera's father) do in the dream (they were suicides in life as well). Another dream with a cave as locale allows Claiborne again to confront reality, the dream already discussed in which Catherine Pollard helps him to see the truth about himself and Vera. He finds her praying in Saint Eustace's chapel, just as he had seen her in the cave of his dream. This chapel is the cavern toward which his essential being had been bearing him, in spite of his being detained in other caves along his pilgrim's way. Here he receives from Catherine the kiss of Christ. In her counsel to him, moreover, the structural lines of the novel converge. The uneasy marriage of Claiborne and Vera yielded to division; but now, with Catherine's blessing, Claiborne wishes a firmer union with Vera than he has known before.

In this novel as in her others, Caroline Gordon reaches a just balance between the idea and the fact, the abstract and the concrete, the metaphysical and the physical. Her novels and short stories take us in a speculative direction and enlarge upon issues that are intellectual and spiritual. But always the abstraction has its basis in the people and the circumstances of the world as she has known it. In her mind and art she has weighed dispassionately the claims of intuition and intelligence, and has been her own best interpreter of the voices that she has heard. In her work sensibility and intellect reach that dynamic equilibrium in which the one faculty strengthens the other. This constantly controlled inspiration of hers accounts, too, for the even quality and the consistent excellence of her books.

Qualities that we associate with the southern mind dominate Miss Gordon as they do writers as various as William Faulkner, Eudora Welty, and Robert Penn Warren. Like these distinguished contemporaries of hers, she has made creative use of the tragic dimensions of human life, the aborted aspirations of most human beings, the sense of evil infecting the good and true, the glories and the burdens of a legendary past, the sense of cultures and individuals in conflict, and a feeling for place that becomes a muted passion.

It is the strength of Miss Gordon's work to suggest continually new facets of significance as one lives through the books in his mind. The characters and the incidents form new configurations with the result that the significance of any one of her books enlarges constantly as one reviews it. Her purpose has been from the beginning to suggest that reality is spiritual as well as empiric, immaterial as well as material. Accordingly, she has presented the experience of her characters in time and then again as it reaches beyond time. The ineffable dimensions of her materials she suggests through a discerning use of myth; and in her later books Christianity reinforces their universal implications. In the first instance, however, her books are faithful to the requirements of art, no matter where they lead philosophically. Only in the most general sense, then, are the books doctrinal. As a writer Miss Gordon is the inquiring moralist even before she is the religious writer. Because of her passionate concern with the way life should be, her books are rooted in social realities even as they look toward the visionary. Intelligence, compassion, psychological insight, depth of vision, and stylistic distinction inform a canon of work that impresses always by its comprehensiveness and strength.

↙ Selected Bibliography

Works of Caroline Gordon

NOVELS AND COLLECTIONS OF SHORT STORIES

Penhally. New York: Scribner's, 1931.

Aleck Maury Sportsman. New York: Scribner's, 1934.

The Garden of Adonis. New York: Scribner's, 1937.

None Shall Look Back. New York: Scribner's, 1937.

Green Centuries. New York: Scribner's, 1941.

The Women on the Porch. New York: Scribner's, 1944.

The Forest of the South. New York: Scribner's, 1945. (Contains "The Captive," "Hear the Nightingale Sing," "The Forest of the South," "The Ice House," "The Burning Eyes," "To Thy Chamber Window, Sweet," "One More Time," "The Last Day in the Field," "Old Red," "Tom Rivers," "The Long Day," "Summer Dust," "Mr. Powers," "Her Quaint Honour," "The Enemies," "The Brilliant Leaves," and "All Lovers Love the Spring.")

The Strange Children. New York: Scribner's, 1951.

The Malefactors. New York: Scribner's, 1956.

Old Red and Other Stories. New York: Scribner's, 1963. (Contains "One Against Thebes," "Emmanuele! Emmanuele!" "The Brilliant Leaves," "All Lovers Love the Spring," "Tom Rivers," "The Petrified Woman," "Old Red," "One More Time," "The Last Day in the Field," "The Presence," "The Ice House," "Hear the Nigtingale Sing," and "The Captive.")

NONFICTION

The House of Fiction: An Anthology of the Short Story, with Commentary by Caroline Gordon and Allen Tate. New York: Scribner's, 1950; second edition, 1960. (Incorporates much of the material in Miss Gordon's previously published critical articles.)

"Some Readings and Misreadings," *Sewanee Review,* 61:384–407 (Summer 1953).

"The Art and Mystery of Faith," *Newman Annual,* 1953, pp. 55–62.

"Mr. Verver, Our National Hero," *Sewanee Review,* 63:29–47 (Winter 1955).

How to Read a Novel. New York: Viking Press, 1957.

"Flannery O'Connor's *Wise Blood,*" *Critique,* 2:3–10 (Fall 1958).

"The Novels of Brainard Cheney," *Sewanee Review,* 67:322–30 (Spring 1959).

A Good Soldier: A Key to the Novels of Ford Madox Ford. Davis: University of California Library, 1963.

Selected Bibliography

CURRENT AMERICAN REPRINTS

How to Read a Novel. New York: Compass Books (Viking Press). $1.45.
The House of Fiction. 2nd edition. New York: Scribner's. $3.25.

Bibliography

Griscom, Joan. "Bibliography of Caroline Gordon," *Critique*, 1:74–78 (Winter 1956).

Critical and Biographical Studies

Blum, Morgan. "The Shifting Point of View: Joyce's 'The Dead' and Gordon's 'Old Red,' " *Critique*, 1:45–66 (Winter 1956).

Bradbury, John M. *Renaissance in the South: A Critical History of the Literature, 1920–1960.* Chapel Hill: University of North Carolina Press, 1964.

Brown, Ashley. "The Novel as Christian Comedy" in *Reality and Myth: Essays in American Literature in Honor of Richard Croom Beatty*, edited by William E. Walker and Robert L. Welker. Nashville, Tenn.: Vanderbilt University Press, 1964.

Cheney, Brainard. "Caroline Gordon's Ontological Quest," *Renascence*, 16: 3–12 (Fall 1963).

Cowan, Louise. "Nature and Grace in Caroline Gordon," *Critique*, 1:11–27 (Winter 1956).

Eisinger, Chester E. *Fiction of the Forties.* Chicago: University of Chicago Press, 1964.

Ford, Ford Madox. "A Stage in American Literature," *Bookman*, 74:371–76 (December 1931).

Hartman, Carl. "Charades at Benfolly," *Western Review*, 16:322–24.

Heilman, Robert B. "School for Girls," *Sewanee Review*, 60:293–304.

Hoffman, Frederick J. "Caroline Gordon: The Special Yield," *Critique*, 1: 29–35 (Winter 1956).

King, Lawrence T. "The Novels of Caroline Gordon," *Catholic World*, 181: 274–79 (July 1955).

Koch, Vivienne. "The Forest of the South," *Sewanee Review*, 54:543–47 (July–September 1946).

————. "The Conservatism of Caroline Gordon," in *Southern Renascence,* edited by Louis D. Rubin and Robert D. Jacobs. Baltimore: Johns Hopkins Press, 1953.

————. "Companions in the Blood," *Sewanee Review*, 64:645–51 (Autumn 1956).

Lytle, Andrew N. "Caroline Gordon and the Historic Image," *Sewanee Review*, 57:560–86 (Autumn 1949).

_____. "The Forest of the South," *Critique*, 1:3–9 (Winter 1956).

O'Connor, William Van. "Art and Miss Gordon" in *The Grotesque: An American Genre and Other Essays*. Carbondale: Southern Illinois University Press, 1962.

Ross, Danforth. "Caroline Gordon's Golden Ball," *Critique*, 1:67–73 (Winter 1956).

Stewart, John L. *The Burden of Time: The Fugitives and Agrarians*. Princeton, N.J.: Princeton University Press, 1965.

Sullivan, Walter. "Southern Novelists and the Civil War" in *Southern Renascence*, edited by Louis D. Rubin and Robert D. Jacobs. Baltimore: Johns Hopkins Press, 1953.

Thorp, Willard. "The Way Back and the Way Up: The Novels of Caroline Gordon," *Bucknell Review*, 6:1–15 (December 1956).

UNIVERSITY OF MINNESOTA
PAMPHLETS ON AMERICAN WRITERS

William Van O'Connor, Allen Tate, Leonard Unger, and Robert Penn Warren, editors. Willard Thorp, Karl Shapiro, and Philip Rahv, advisers

EACH PAMPHLET, 65 CENTS

UNIVERSITY OF MINNESOTA PRESS, Minneapolis, Minnesota 55455, U.S.A.